published
and
funded by

Humanities Iowa

Iowa Lewis & Clark
Bicentennial Commission

with assistance from

Golden Hills Resource Conservation &
Development

Western Iowa Tourism Region

Iowa West Foundation

CAPTAIN LEWIS.

CAPTAIN CLARKE.

Captain Lewis, Dayton, O.B.F. Ellis, 1840, Yale
Collection of Western Americana, Beinecke Rare
Book and Manuscript Library

Captain Clark, Dayton, O.B.F. Ellis, 1840, Yale
Collection of Western Americana, Beinecke Rare
Book and Manuscript Library

Lewis and Clark in Iowa

Clay S. Jenkinson

Cover image: Continuation of January 17-20, 1804,
two drawings of the keelboat (detail), William Clark
Field Notes, Yale Collection of Western Americana,
Beinecke Rare Book and Manuscript Library

ISBN 0-9753751-0-5

A Note on the Artificiality of State Boundaries

When Lewis and Clark ascended the Missouri River in the summer of 1804, they could not anticipate the state boundaries that would eventually be imposed on the 828,000 square miles of the Louisiana Purchase. During the thirty-nine days that they spent on the stretch of the Missouri River along what is now Iowa, they had no idea that they were exploring what would become the border between Iowa (admitted 1846, the twenty-ninth state) and Nebraska (1867, the thirty-seventh state). In the course of those thirty-nine days (thirty-four days in 1804, five in 1806), they spent about an equal amount of time in what is now Nebraska and what is now Iowa. Their choice of campsites had nothing to do with modern jurisdictions. They simply chose the best campsite that appeared at the time when the expedition needed to stop forward progress for the night. Sometimes they chose their campsites to enable them to make contact with the Indian peoples of the region, who lived principally on the Nebraska side of the Missouri River. At other times, they chose stopping places that would enable the captains to conduct celestial observations in their quest to determine the latitude and longitude of key places on the river.

Any study of Lewis and Clark in Iowa is necessarily a study of Lewis and Clark in Iowa and Nebraska. This chapbook makes no attempt to prefer Iowa over Nebraska, focus on Iowa events to the exclusion of Nebraska, or pretend that events that occurred in today's Nebraska occurred in Iowa. This chapbook's general focus on Iowa has more to do with the location of the institutions that commissioned it, and paid for it, than with any geographic parochialism.

It is always essential to remember that Lewis and Clark thought they were traveling along one of the middle stretches of the Missouri River in Thomas Jefferson's Louisiana Purchase territory. They were prior to, and above, state pride.

Lewis and Clark in Iowa

What Happened on the Lewis and Clark Expedition in Iowa?

Four significant events occurred during the period that the Corps of Discovery spent in or just across the river from what is now Iowa.

First, Sergeant Charles Floyd died of natural causes on August 20, 1804. Although the captains could not know it at the time, Floyd would be the only member of the Lewis and Clark Expedition to die in the course of the journey.

Second, the expedition reached and passed the mouth of the Platte River. The Platte represented a line of demarcation between the lower and upper Missouri River. In crossing the confluence of the Platte and Missouri Rivers, the expedition moved from the central prairies of America to the Great Plains, a geographic region quite different from anything they had previously experienced.

Third, in what is now Iowa (and Nebraska), Lewis and Clark had their first significant encounters with Native Americans. Their encounters with the Oto and Missouri at a Nebraska benchland they called the Council Bluff (near today's Fort Calhoun) and later at Fish Camp (near today's Dakota City, Nebraska) inaugurated one of President Jefferson's prime objectives for the expedition.

Fourth, the Corps of Discovery endured its gravest discipline crisis of the entire journey.

On August 18, 1804, Meriwether Lewis's thirtieth birthday, U.S. Army private Moses Reed was courtmartialed for desertion.

All this, and much more, occurred along the 342 mile corridor of the Missouri River that forms the western boundary of Iowa.

How Much Time Did Lewis and Clark Spend in Iowa?

The Corps of Discovery passed through the western edge of what is now Iowa twice, once in 1804 during the expedition's first year of travel, and again in 1806 on the journey home. In 1804, the expedition entered today's Iowa on July 18, 1804, and left Iowa on August 21, 1804 (34 days). The return visit was much more brief, of course, because the expedition was floating down the Missouri River with a much diminished payload. In 1806, the expedition entered what is now Iowa on September 4, and left the state for the final time on September 9 (five days).

Iowa became the 29th state on December 28, 1846, forty years after Lewis and Clark passed through on their return journey.

Lewis and Clark in Iowa: Day by Day/Distance Covered

1804

July 18 Expedition passes bluff on the Iowa shore that had fallen away from the river hills. A stray Indian dog hovers near the camp. Forward progress: 18 miles, camp in Nebraska.

July 19 The landscape is so beautiful that Clark forgets the purpose of his time on the shore. 10 3/4 miles, camp on island in the middle of the river.

July 20 The expedition reaches Weeping Water Creek. 18 miles, camp in Nebraska.

July 21 The expedition reaches the mouth of the Platte River. The captains ascend the Platte a small distance to reconnoiter. 19 miles, camp in Nebraska.

July 22 Expedition establishes Camp White Catfish on the Iowa side of the river. 10 miles, camp in Iowa.

July 23 Captains send Drouillard and Cruzatte to make contact with the Oto and Missouri Indians. No forward progress, camp in Iowa.

July 24 The captains prepare reports and maps to send to the President of the United States. No forward progress, camp in Iowa.

July 25 Drouillard and Cruzatte return having made no contact with the Oto, Missouri or Pawnee. No forward progress, camp in Iowa.

July 26 Clark flees to the woods to avoid a sandstorm while working on his map of the Missouri. No forward progress, camp in Iowa.

July 27 Expedition gets underway again after five nights in the same camp. Clark walks on shore with Reubin Field to examine what he takes to be Indian burial mounds. 15 miles, camp in Nebraska.

July 28 Drouillard makes contact with a Missouri Indian while hunting on the shore. 10 3/4 miles, camp below the point of an island, Iowa.

July 29 La Liberté and the Missouri Indian are sent out to the Oto and Missouri village. 12 miles, camp in Iowa.

July 30 Expedition reaches and establishes camp at the Council Bluff. A stray Indian horse traveling with the expedition dies. 3 1/4 miles, camp in Nebraska.

July 31 Reubin and Joseph Field lose the expedition's two horses while hunting. No forward progress, camp in Nebraska.

August 1 William Clark's 34th birthday. Men sent out in search of the lost horses. No forward progress, camp in Nebraska.

August 2 The Oto and Missouri delegation comes in the company of a French trader named Fairfong. The lost horses are recovered. No forward progress, camp in Nebraska.

August 3 The expedition's first council with American Indians. 5 miles, camp in Nebraska.

August 4 The captains realize that Moses Reed has disappeared and perhaps deserted. 15 miles, camp in Nebraska.

August 5 The Moses Reed crisis grows. 20 1/2 miles, camp in Iowa.

August 6 The captains determine to send out a four-man search party to bring Reed back dead or alive. 20 1/2 miles, camp in Iowa.

August 7 The "posse" sets out, carrying written instructions, authorizing them to put Reed to death if necessary. 18 miles, camp in Iowa.

August 8 Expedition comes upon immense quantities of floating pelican feathers near the mouth of the Little Sioux River. 16 miles, camp in Iowa.

August 9 After being detained by fog in the morning, the expedition circumnavigates a gigantic oxbow. 17 1/2 miles, camp in Nebraska.

August 10 Expedition reaches Blackbird Hill, named for a famous and powerful Omaha leader.

22 1/4 miles, camp on willow island near the Iowa shore.

August 11 Captains ascend Blackbird Hill with a small party and leave a white flag bordered in red and blue as a gesture of respect. 17 1/2 miles, camp in Nebraska.

August 12 One man steps wades across a huge oxbow while the boats labor around it. It was 18 3/4 miles around and just 974 yards across. 20 1/4 miles, camp on sand island on the Iowa side of the river.

August 13 Sergeant Ordway and others dispatched to try to make contact with the Omaha Indians. 17 miles, camp in Nebraska.

August 14 Ordway and his party return to report that the Omaha village is deserted. No forward progress, camp in Nebraska.

August 15 Clark goes fishing with a fish drag. Captain Lewis sends Pierre Dorion and others to determine whether a prairie fire is a signal set by the Sioux Indians. No forward progress, camp in Nebraska.

August 16 Lewis leads a fishing party and brings back more than 800 fish. No forward progress, camp in Nebraska.

August 17 One member of the party returns to report that Reed has been captured, but that La Liberté managed to escape; and that Oto and Missouri leaders are on their way to camp. No forward progress, camp in Nebraska.

August 18 Meriwether Lewis's 30th birthday. Moses Reed tried and punished for desertion. No forward progress, camp in Nebraska.

August 19 Expedition holds council with Oto and Missouri leaders Little Thief and Big Horse.

Sergeant Charles Floyd struck by sudden illness. No forward progress, camp in Nebraska.

August 20   Charles Floyd dies. He is buried on a bluff on the Iowa shore with full military honors. 13 miles, camp in Iowa.

August 21   Expedition reaches Big Sioux River. 22 3/4 miles, camp in Nebraska.

August 22   Corps moves upstream from the land that would become Iowa. 19 miles.

1806

September 4   After obtaining flour and tobacco from trader James Aird, the expedition moves on to Floyd's Bluff. The captains and some of the men visit and restore Floyd's grave. 36 miles, camp in Nebraska.

September 5   The oppressiveness of the mosquitos inspires the men to get into the boats sooner than expected. 73 miles, camp in Iowa.

September 6   The captains buy whiskey from a trader named Henry Delorn. Some of the men exchange their buckskin attire for linen shirts and coarse woven hats. 30 miles, camp in Iowa.

September 7   After re-establishing contact with the Field brothers after they had been absent hunting, the expedition has a sumptuous feast of elk flesh. 44 miles, camp in Nebraska.

September 8   After strenuous rowing that carried the expedition 78 miles, the expedition establishes camp at Camp White Catfish north of the Platte River. 78 miles, camp in Iowa.

September 9   The expedition passes the mouth of the Platte River. Clark reports that Meriwether Lewis has fully recovered from his gunshot wounds of August 11. Late in the day the expedition passes out of Iowa and camps in Missouri at the Bald-Pated Prairie. 73 miles, camp in Missouri.

How Was the Expedition Traveling in Iowa?

In July and August, 1804, the expedition's flotilla consisted of three boats. The principal vessel was a fifty-five foot keelboat that Captain Lewis had had constructed for the expedition in Pittsburgh at the head of the Ohio River. It contained most of the baggage of the expedition. It could accommodate twenty-two oarsmen. The rest of the fleet consisted of two large pirogues, a red pirogue manned by French *engagés* and a white pirogue manned by a handful of the expedition's enlisted men. A pirogue is a long flat-bottomed boat.

At this point the expedition had two horses, which were used for hunting along the shores of the Missouri River. At one point the expedition had possessed four horses. Only two were still alive during the Iowa phase of the expedition.

How Many Men Were Traveling with Lewis and Clark in Iowa?

Approximately fifty. The expedition started out with the two captains (Clark was actually only a lieutenant, but he was called captain by everyone, including Meriwether Lewis), three sergeants (Nathaniel Pryor, Charles Floyd, John Ordway), and twenty-four privates. That makes a total of twenty-nine in what would later be called the "permanent party." In addition, at least eight French *engagés* were assigned to the red pirogue, and Corporal Richard Warfington led a detachment of five men who would constitute the core of the return party that brought the expedition's keelboat back from Fort Mandan at the end of the winter of 1804-1805. These groups total 43, but it is certain that the expedition traveled with more men than that. Among other things, there is some uncertainty about which individuals belonged to which group, and the captains were less concerned to count the French watermen than the officially enlisted Army personnel. The French watermen were seen as "porters" of the expedition. They appear to have dined, slept, worked, and played somewhat apart from the main party, and they seldom appear by name in the expedition's journals.

What Did the Expedition Eat in Iowa?

Deer and elk mostly. And no buffalo.

The expedition did not kill its first buffalo until August 23, 1804, just after it entered what is now South Dakota.

On July 26, Clark reported that five beaver had been caught near Camp White Catfish, "the flesh of which we made use of." Beaver were plentiful along the Iowa-Nebraska corridor. In fact, Clark commented in surprise that the local Indians seemed not to hunt them whatsoever.

During periods of relative leisure, the Lewis and Clark Expedition went a'fishing. At what Clark called Fish Camp on the Nebraska shore on August 15, 1804, Clark and ten men ventured to a creek and managed to catch 318 fish with a makeshift fish drag. The catch included pike, bass, perch, catfish, shorthead red horse, and freshwater drum, among others, and shrimp and mussels. The shrimp, Clark noted, were "prosisely of Shape Size & flavour of those about

N. Orleans & the lower party of the Mississippi."
The next day Captain Lewis took a party back
to the same river and brought in more than 800
fish, 490 of which were catfish. Undoubtedly the
men of the expedition enjoyed these feasts of
fresh fish as a break from their otherwise all-red-
meat diet, but the journals indicate that the men
generally preferred red meat to fish, even when
that meant purchasing herds of Indian dogs in the
Columbia River valley.

The expedition also reports the consumption of
wild turkeys, geese, and pelican in Iowa, though
not in quantities sufficient to satisfy the hunger
of nearly fifty hard-working young men. Because
they passed through Iowa in late summer or early
fall in both 1804 and 1806, Corps members were
able to harvest wild fruit on a regular basis: wild
black currants, choke cherries, wild grapes, wild
plums, wolfberry, western snowberry, and wild
raspberries. On one occasion, July 19, 1804,
according to journal keeper John Ordway, "we
gethered a quantity of [choke] cherries at noon
time & put in to the Whisky barrel." That must
have been quite a night!

Because the expedition was still relatively close
to St. Charles, its larders still contained a number
of items, in Lewis's phrase, "which the hand of
civilization has prepared for us." Clark reported
that the last of the butter was consumed on July
19, 1804, and he noted on July 18, 1804, that the
expedition still had a supply of coffee.

On the return journey in 1806, the expedition
managed to purchase a barrel of flour from
the Scottish trader James Aird just as it re-
entered today's Iowa. At that time Clark reports
(astonishingly) that the expedition still had a small

... in great quantities in the Columbia R.
...t 40 miles above us by means of skiming
cooping nets. on this page I have drawn
likeness of them as large as life; it
...erfect as I can make it with my
...and will serve to give a
...ral idea of the fish. the
...s of the fins are boney but
...sharp tho' somewhat pointed.
...small fin on the back
...t to the tail has no
...s of bone being a
...anous pellicle.
...he gills have
... those of the
...t each, those
...20 and 2
...of the back
...fins are of
...t a bleuish
...the lower
...t a silve=
...t. the
...d the
...nd of
...uple
...ver

thin .
the fins
eleven ra
abdomen h
of the pinna
haff formed in
has eleven rays. a
a white colour. the
duskey colour and that
part of the sides and b
-ng white. no spots on
first bone of the gills
eye is of a bleuis cast; and t
a light goald colour nearly n
of the eye is black and the iris
white. the under jaw exceeds the u
the mouth opens to great extent, fol
that of the herring. it has no teeth
the abdomen is obtuse and smooth; in the
differing from the herring, shad anchovy
&c of the Malacapterygious Order & Class
Clupea

Lewis and Clark Codex J:93 (Eulachon)
American Philosophical Society

13

quantity of the flour with which it set off from St. Louis twenty-eight months previously!

At no point in what is now Iowa could anyone declare, as did Meriwether Lewis in the Bitterroot Mountains, that he was "hungary as a wolf."

Was All of Iowa Included in the Louisiana Purchase?

Every acre. What the United States purchased from Napoleon in 1803 was the entire watershed of the Missouri River. Another way of describing the Louisiana Purchase is that it added to the United States the west bank of the Mississippi River all the way to the continental divide. Although Spain contested the United States' notion of the southern and southwestern boundaries of the Louisiana Purchase, and there was some uncertainty about the northern boundaries west of the putative source of the Mississippi River and the Lake of the Woods, the core of the Louisiana Purchase was entirely uncontested—American—ground. The entire state of Iowa falls within the boundaries of the Louisiana Purchase. Iowa is unique in that its eastern and western boundaries are formed by two of North America's great rivers, the Mississippi on the east and the Missouri (and Big Sioux) on the west.

How Far Did Lewis and Clark Venture from the Missouri River?

Not far. President Jefferson's instructions called for Lewis to "explore the Missouri river, & such principal stream of it, as, by it's course & communication with the waters of the Pacific Ocean, may offer the most direct & practicable water communication across this continent, for the purposes of commerce." It was a very rare occasion when any member of the Lewis and Clark Expedition ventured more than a few miles from the rivers on which they traveled across the continent.

What Are Some of the "Firsts" Associated with Lewis and Clark in Iowa and Nebraska?

They held their first formal Indian council, with a small group of Oto and Missouri leaders, at the Council Bluff, on August 3, 1804, and with a more important group of leaders on August 19, 1804 near Dakota City, Nebraska. Since both of these parleys were with leaders of the Oto and Missouri tribes, they may be seen as the same council conducted in two venues.

As a result of this council, Lewis and Clark suffered their first diplomatic setback in the course of the expedition. When a sub-leader rejected a paper certificate of good behavior, considering it a gift insufficient to his importance, and even Little Thief and Big Horse made it clear that they could not be expected to promote the expedition's peace, trade, and harmony agenda without very substantial gifts, Lewis and Clark were indignant, but they must also have realized that Mr. Jefferson's blithe optimism about Indian relations was going to have to yield to the social, traditional, geopolitical, and economic realities of Indian country.

The first (and only) death of an expedition member occurred during the Iowa interlude. Charles Floyd died of natural causes at noon on August 20, 1804.

That means also that Floyd was the first member of the expedition to die. The second was probably Joseph Field, who seems to have died in 1807, less than a year after his homecoming. Ironically, the last expedition member to die was the man who replaced Floyd as sergeant, Patrick Gass. He died on April 2, 1870 at the age of 99.

They saw their first coyote on August 12, 1804. They did not actually kill a coyote until September 18, 1804.

Meriwether Lewis prepared the expedition's first taxidermical sample in Iowa. On June 30, 1804, Joseph Field killed and brought in a badger (*Taxidea taxus taxus*). Except for a couple of French *engagés*, nobody had ever seen one before. Just at this time the captains were preparing written materials to send back to President Jefferson. Although in the end the dispatch boat was never sent, Lewis appears to have spent the last days of July making a taxidermical reconstruction of the creature. In his usual matter-of-fact way, Clark wrote, "We have this animale Skined and Stuffed." The stuffed badger eventually made its way from Fort Mandan in North Dakota to St. Louis on the expedition's keelboat, and then was shipped via New Orleans and the Atlantic coastal passage to Baltimore and Washington, D.C. We know that President Jefferson received the badger because he wrote about it in a letter to his scientist friend C.F.C. Volney.

How Was the Health of the Expedition in Iowa?

Aside from the sudden death of Charles Floyd, the expedition was mostly healthy in what is now Iowa.

On July 20, Clark wrote, "It is wothey of observation to mention that our party has been much healtier on the Voyage than parites of the

Same Number is in any other Situation." Clark also noted that "Tumers have been troublesom to them all." By tumors Clark meant boils.

On July 26, Clark drained an abscess on the chest of one of the men (unnamed), discharging half a pint of fluid and providing the individual considerable relief.

In late July, Joseph Whitehouse cut himself in the knee, "verry bad," said William Clark. Whitehouse himself wrote, "I cut my [text illegible] on the 27 [of July] had to Lay By my ower [he was excused from rowing duty] the Cout [cut] was one inch and a half Long."

The indispensable George Drouillard was described as "Sick" on July 20, but it could not have been too serious, because he was able to undertake a diplomatic mission just three days later.

On July 29, Clark noted that there were "two men Sick & Several with Boils."

On the return journey in 1806, the chief medical concern was the recovery of Captain Meriwether Lewis from an accidental gunshot wound to the buttocks on August 11. Clark reported that Lewis was well enough on September 4 to climb up the hill to Charles Floyd's grave. By September 9, Lewis was pronounced to be fully recovered. Thus ended happily a gun accident that might have terminated Lewis's life and changed the course of American history.

How Did the Journal Keepers Respond to the Landscape of Iowa and Nebraska?

Unfortunately, Meriwether Lewis was essentially silent through the whole Iowa-Nebraska interlude, both in 1804 and 1806. Generally speaking, Lewis was the best writer of the expedition. His journal entries are richly detailed, thoughtful, sometimes lyrical, and at times philosophical. When Lewis was keeping his journal, his entries are almost always the most interesting of the lot, and the ones most likely to slip into revery. Lewis's only known response to the Iowa landscape was his description of the confluence of the Platte and Missouri Rivers, which is justly famous.

On the whole, William Clark was much more matter of fact and down to earth than his partner in discovery Meriwether Lewis. And yet he was so taken by the scale and beauty of the Nebraska and Iowa landscape that he found himself gushing. The most remarkable of his half-dozen paeans to the beauty of the middle-Missouri landscape was written just inside what is now Iowa airspace. Clark wrote: "after assending and passing thro a narrow Strip of wood Land, Came Suddenly into an open and bound less Prarie, I Say bound less because I could not See the extent of the plain in any Derection, the timber appeared to be confined to the River Creeks & Small branches, this Prarie was Covered with grass about 18 Inches or 2 feat high and contained little of any thing else, except as before mentioned on the River Creeks &c, This prospect was So Sudden & entertaining that I forgot the object of my prosute and turned my attention to the Variety which presented themselves to my view."

On the return journey, perhaps because the expedition was moving at least three times as fast as on the 1804 ascent, Clark pauses several times to comment on the character of the Missouri River. Above the Platte, he writes, the river's path is much more serpentine and curvaceous, and more beset with snags and other impediments.

The lesser journal keepers, Patrick Gass, Joseph Whitehouse, Charles Floyd, and John Ordway all wrote about the beauty of the Iowa and Nebraska landscape. Joseph Whitehouse's August 21, 1804, journal entry is representative: "The Country here is very Rich Priari land, having very high Grass on it; and at the farther side of the River, it has some Trees growing on it & affords a pleasant view.—"

What is Revealed about the Character of Meriwether Lewis and William Clark in Iowa?

The journals for this period reveal that the expedition had settled into an efficient routine. The authority of the expedition's leaders was sure and almost entirely unquestioned. The shared command (the fictional co-captaincy of Lewis and Clark) appears to have presented no difficulties to the nearly fifty men of the expedition. The two leaders had already settled into their characteristic roles: Clark seems to have been handling the day to day business of getting the flotilla up the Missouri River. Lewis was the expedition's naturalist, astronomer, philosopher, and final arbiter. Clark kept the captains' log. Lewis played a more fluid role in pursuit of the Enlightenment goals for the expedition. If Lewis's journal silence is bewildering, Clark's effusions about the beauty of the Iowa and Nebraska landscape are charming and endearing. From all appearances, the partnership between Lewis and Clark appears to have been easy, natural, and relaxed.

Clark took great pride in his ability with firearms, and throughout the journals he exhibits a reluctance to acknowledge that he might simply have missed a shot. During the Iowa period, the stakes were not high as food was plentiful, but Clark could not admit that he might simply have missed the elk he was stalking. On August 8, 1804, he wrote, "Collin Killed an elk, I fired 4 times at one & have reasons to think I Kiled him but could not find him." A sentence or so later, Clark hints at a more rational explanation: "The Misqutors were So troublesom and Misqutors thick in the Plains that I could not Keep them out of my eyes, with a bush."

One of the most interesting elements in the character of William Clark is his propensity to believe that whenever there was a cultural misunderstanding with the Indians the expedition encountered, his second, more detailed explanation of the ways and means of the Corps of Discovery was automatically satisfying to his Indian hosts. This pattern of believing that skeptical Indians always and automatically accepted the Corps of Discovery's explanations of its principles occurred many times in the course of the expedition. Clark never once concluded that the Indians were simply unconvinced by his explanations, and he never conceded the slightest recognition that one culture's ways are frequently incomprehensible (or barbaric) to another, and that it may well have been the case that the Indians' concerns were just. In some regards Clark was more optimistic than the patron of the expedition, Thomas Jefferson.

Although Meriwether Lewis appears not to have kept a regular journal during the

Iowa interlude, he was busy making celestial observations, collecting plant and animal specimens, and writing about new and unusual animal species. The absence of a regular journal throws into relief those entries that Lewis did produce, all of which (in Iowa) belong to the category of natural science. Lewis's journal entries exhibit a deep curiosity about the natural world, the minute discernment of his eye, and his extraordinary attention to detail. Although President Jefferson conceded that Lewis was "not regularly educated," he realized that his protégé had extraordinary powers of observation coupled with the ability to articulate his impressions on paper.

When U.S. Army private Moses Reed deserted the expedition in August, 1804, the captains exhibited a combination of anger, vindictiveness, and concern for due process and the rule of military law. On August 7, 1804, they sent out a four-man party of their ablest and most reliable men with instructions to bring in Reed dead or alive. They were not about to permit Reed to slip away onto the Great Plains with impunity. They knew that the long-term *esprit de corps* of the expedition depended on a firm and unambiguous response to the Reed crisis. Even so, Clark notes that in instructing the "posse" to put Reed to death, if necessary, the captains "als[o] gave pointed orders to the party in writeing." In other words, the captains provided written instructions so that, in the event of the "posse" putting Reed to death, the four individuals would be protected from criticism or legal prosecution for their actions. The captains, Meriwether Lewis and William Clark, were taking full responsibility for the severity of their orders. They were leaving no room for ambiguity.

How Did Camp White Catfish Get its Name?

On July 23, 1804, William Clark reported that "one of the men cought a white Catfish, the eyes Small, & Tale resembling that of a Dolfin." The individual was Silas Goodrich, who is known to history principally as the expedition's fisherman. The naturalist Paul Russell Cutright, who characterized Goodrich as the Izaak Walton of the expedition, concluded that what he caught was a channel catfish. If this is true, Lewis and Clark discovered the species. Camp White Catfish was on the Iowa side of the Missouri, near the Mills and Pottawattamie county line. The expedition spent five nights at the site, the first sustained period of rest for the enlisted men and French *engagés* since the journey began on May 14, 1804.

How Did the Council Bluff Get its Name?

The Council Bluff was the name given to the site of the Lewis and Clark Expedition's first formal council with Native Americans.

Lewis and Clark originally expected to hold a council with the Oto and Missouri Indians at what they called Camp White Catfish. They sent George Drouillard and Pierre Cruzatte up the Platte on July 23-25, 1804 to make contact with the Oto and Missouri and bring a delegation back to the Missouri River. That initiative came to nothing. A few days later, they renewed their

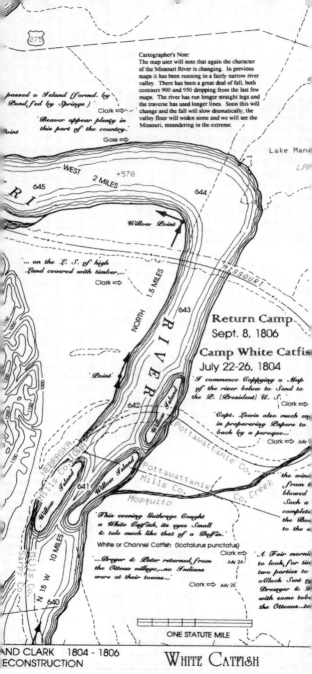

attempt to find Indians with whom to hold a
council, but because they did not wish to hold
up progress of the expedition, they told the
emissaries that they would form a council camp
"at the next bend of High Land on the L.S. [i.e., the
Nebraska shore]. They came to a perfect council
site on July 30.

Expedition journal keeper Joseph Whitehouse
provided an excellent description of the site: "The
morning still continued Cloudy, we set out early,
and passed a high bottom Priari on the North
Side; having on the back side of them high ridges
with Trees growing on them. above the bottom
Priari the hills make in close to the river; and are
very high and steep, we passed the Mouth of
a Creek, laying on the North side of the River,
which is called knob Creek."

What Lewis and Clark found near Fort Calhoun,
Nebraska, was not only a good council site, but
as later events of the nineteenth century would
confirm, one of the best natural meeting and
fortification sites on the central Missouri River.

Patrick Gass was the first member of the
expedition to use the term Council Bluff, on
July 30, 1804. Clark first employed the term
"Camp Councile Bluff" in his journal entry for
August 3, 1804.

The actual site of the council has probably been
washed away by the Missouri River. In 1969
Paul Russell Cutright wrote, "It is impossible to
determine the precise location of this site today
since flood waters have seemingly long since
carried it to sea."

Today's city of Council Bluffs, Iowa, is
approximately fifteen miles south of the 1804
council.

What Features of the Landscape Did Lewis and Clark Name in Iowa?

Not many. Most of the creeks and prominent landscape features of the Missouri River between St. Charles and the Yellowstone River in the northwestern corner of today's North Dakota had been named by the time Lewis and Clark arrived. French and Spanish explorers and traders had given names to the features of the Missouri River valley, and Lewis and Clark tended to accept most of that nomenclature as established. Compared to other explorers, Lewis and Clark were quite conservative and respectful in their naming procedures.

According to Paul Russell Cutright, the expedition named nine landscape features in what is now Iowa and Nebraska. Bald-Pated Prairie, Council Bluffs, the Floyd River, and Floyds Bluff still retain their expedition-derived names, with slight variations. The original "Sergts. Floyds Bluff" has long since fallen into the voracious Missouri River and made its way to the Gulf of Mexico.

Among the Indians

How Did the Expedition Make Contact with the Oto and Missouri Indians?

The captains knew they would most likely encounter the Oto and Missouri Indians near the mouth of the Platte River. This information came from traders in St. Louis and from some of the French members of the expedition, chiefly Francois Labiche and Pierre Cruzatte.

When the expedition reached the region near the mouth of the Platte, the captains realized that these semi-agricultural Indians were engaged in their summer buffalo hunt west of the Missouri River on the Nebraska plains. "[A]s those Indians are now out in the Praries following & Hunting the buffalow, I fear we will not see them," Clark wrote on July 20, 1804.

From Camp White Catfish, on July 23, 1804, the captains sent Pierre Cruzatte and George Drouillard up the Platte River to make contact with the Oto and Missouri, and (if possible) the Pawnee Indians. The captains expected to conduct their first council with Indians at Camp White Catfish. They instructed the men of the expedition to put their weapons in order, and they erected a flag above their temporary camp. Drouillard and Cruzatte hiked eighteen, possibly as many as forty-five, miles upriver into today's Nebraska to reach the Oto and Missouri village, found it empty, and returned to the expedition's camp on July 25, 1804. Three days later, Drouillard did encounter a Missouri individual while hunting on the prairie. The Missouri man provided details of the size and whereabouts of the Indian villages near the Platte River mouth. On July 29, the French *engagé* known as La Liberté was sent alone with the Missouri man to make contact with his tribe. La Liberté promptly deserted. On August 1, the captains sent another man out in search of La Liberté: "The Indians not yet arrived we fear Something amiss with our messenger or them," Clark wrote.

Finally, on August 2, 1804, the Oto and Missouri Indians came on their own initiative. They were accompanied by a white trader, whom Clark called Mr. Fairfong. An unspecified number of Oto and Missouri Indians came to the Council Bluff.

What Were the Main Points of Meriwether Lewis's Speeches to the Indians the Expedition Met?

On August 3, 1804, Clark summarized the expedition's intention of "Delivering a Speech informing thos Children of ours of the Change which had taken place, the wishes of our government to Cultivate friendship & good understanding, the method of have good advice & Some Directions." On the same day he clarified this to say: "Delivered a long Speech to them expressive of our journey the wirkes of our Government, Some advice to them and Directions how They were to Conduct themselves."

Lewis and Clark's Indian speeches were characterized by six themes:

1. Captain Lewis explained that the United States had purchased the Louisiana country and in so doing had pre-empted Spain, France, and Britain in that district. The former French and Spanish sovereigns were leaving the territory, Lewis explained, and they were never coming back.

2. The Lewis and Clark Expedition was not a trading party and it did not wish to engage in trade with the Indians it met. It was true that the expedition's boats were heavily loaded with industrial tools, scientific instruments, and goods, but most of these materials were for internal use by the expedition and those items it had brought for Indians were intended as gifts, and as a kind of menu of the kind of trade goods that would follow in the wake of the expedition.

3. The Indians of the Louisiana Territory were encouraged to live in peace with each other, and in particular with their new American friends. If they would agree to put down the war hatchet,

and cease their incessant war skirmishing, they might live in peace and prosperity under the security umbrella of the United States government.

4.Indian refusal to listen to the wisdom of the great white father would result in economic strangulation and—in extreme circumstances—war. Any attempts to interfere with or molest white traders would be dealt with severely. Indian cooperation with the expedition's purposes and progress would hasten the time when a reliable and steady supply of American trade goods reached their villages.

5.President Jefferson strongly encouraged Indian tribes to send delegations to Washington, D.C., to confer with him. All expenses would be paid, and members of such delegations could expect lavish gifts.

6.If tribes wished some of their children to travel to St. Louis or other American cities to be educated in the white man's way, the captains would be happy to make arrangements, and President Jefferson would be very pleased.

What Sort of Gifts Did Lewis and Clark Give the Oto and Missouri Indians?

At the first council, on August 3, 1804, Clark said the expedition sent a "flag Meadel & Some Cloathes," to the absent leader Little Thief, who was away hunting. To the lesser leaders who actually attended the first council, the captains presented "a Cannister of Powder [and a corresponding quantity of lead ball] and a Bottle of whiskey and delivered a few presents to the whole after giving a Br: Cth: [breech cloth] Some Paint [vermillion] guartering [garter material]."

Captains Lewis & Clark holding a Council with the Indians

Captain Lewis and Clark holding a council with
the Indians, illustration by Patrick Gass, 1810,
Yale Collection of Western Americana, Beinecke
Rare Book and Manuscript Library

The expedition carried several types of U.S. government peace medals. The majority were Jefferson Peace Medals in three sizes, with the face of Jefferson on one side, and a tomahawk, pipe, and the clasped hands of peace on the obverse face. The motto said "PEACE AND FRIENDSHIP." Other medals, left over from the Washington administration, featured pastoral scenes: a man sowing grain; a shepherd with domestic stock; and a woman spinning cloth. The pastoral (sometimes called season) medals had been designed by the American artist John Trumbull, a friend of Jefferson's.

At the first council the expedition gave two of the leaders who were present medals of the second size and four leaders medals of the third grade. They sent back one of the largest medals for the man they designated "the Grand Chief," Little Thief, and a medal of the second grade for Big Horse.

At the second council, on August 19, 1804, the captains presented a number of unspecified gifts to the Oto and Missouri delegation, and also issued paper certificates of good behavior to a number of individuals, perhaps everyone present.

Clark reported that the Indians "were not well Satisfied with the Presents given them." The Oto leader Big Horse said, frankly, "I came *here* naked and must return home naked." He made it clear that he could not be expected to restrain his young warriors from warring against the Omaha if the captains did not give him substantial gifts to distribute among his tribe.

Indian presents constituted the largest expenditure of the initial $2500 budget for the expedition. Lewis spent $669.50 on such items as needles, awls, knives, scarlet cloth, broaches, combs, handkerchiefs, looking glasses, kettles, curtain rings, lockets, fish hooks, and trade beads. Some variety of these items, surely, passed into the hands of the Oto and Missouri leaders.

What Do We Know about the Oto Chiefs Little Thief and Big Horse?

Little Thief (*We-ar-ruge-nor*) was one of the principal Oto leaders. Clark lists Big Horse (*Shon go ton go*) as an Oto, but historian James Ronda more properly identifies him as a Missouri. The tribes had sufficiently blended by the time Lewis and Clark arrived in 1804 to make such distinctions difficult.

Little Thief and Big Horse were absent from the first council with the Oto and Missouri on August 3, 1804, at the Council Bluff. Two weeks later, they made the considerable journey from their Platte River villages to Fish Camp, which was located not far from today's Dakota City, Nebraska, to hear what Lewis and Clark had to say. The second Oto and Missouri council occurred at Fish Camp on August 19, 1804.

"[T]hose People are all Naked, Covered only with Breech Clouts Blankits or Buffalow Roabes," Clark wrote. One of the leaders, probably Little Thief, "beged for a Sun glass," that is, one of the expedition's magnifying glasses.

Little Thief's response to the expedition's peace, trade, and sovereignty speech was recorded by William Clark. Little Thief said his people had always lived in friendship with French traders, and that the Otos and Missouris lived together in easy harmony. He urged Lewis and Clark to linger in the area long enough to meet a fuller contingent of the Oto tribe. That would enable the captains to meet all of the Oto "men of Consequnce." Little Thief made it clear that he and his followers would appreciate gifts from the expedition's stores, and he announced that they would welcome the receipt of the certificates of good behavior that Lewis and Clark were carrying.

We are fortunate to have Clark's notes recording the main points of Little Thief and Big Horse's speeches at the August 19, 1804, council. The story of the Lewis and Clark Expedition has been told almost exclusively from the Anglo-American point of view. Although the expedition was essentially an encounters story, most of the more than fifty encounters with Native Americans were documented from the point of view of the military visitors, rather than their aboriginal hosts. On those few occasions when Lewis or Clark took time to record what they took to be Indian responses to their visit, a small and imperfect window opens into the larger context of the expedition. While it would be a mistake to assume that Clark's transcription of Little Thief's and Big Horse's speeches is fully accurate, nuanced, and complete, such transcriptions are all we have to work with, and they represent invaluable voices from the history of the American West.

Who was Blackbird and What is his Relation to the Lewis and Clark Expedition?

The great Omaha leader Blackbird (*Wazhi gacabe* or *Washinga Sahba*) was dead by the time the Lewis and Clark Expedition reached the homeland of the Omaha Indians. According to

Clark, he had died in the year 1800 of smallpox, along with four hundred members of his tribe.

Blackbird was a man of great power, friendly to white traders, a remarkably strong leader among his own people. He was said to possess enough medicine to make his enemies disappear as if by magic. Historians believe he used poisons, perhaps arsenic, obtained from St. Louis traders to accomplish these murders. According to legends that precede Lewis and Clark, he was buried at the top of Blackbird Hill seated atop his horse, scanning his mighty domains. Today many Omaha cultural leaders dispute the legend of his burial atop his horse.

What did Sacagawea do in Iowa?

Nothing. Sacagawea did not meet Lewis and Clark until November 11, 1804 in what is now central North Dakota, and she did not join the expedition until its departure from Fort Mandan on April 7, 1805. Although Sacagawea now occupies a central place in the Lewis and Clark story, it is important to remember that she was, in a sense, an accidental hire. Lewis and Clark did not set out from St. Charles believing that they would obtain the services of a seventeen-year-old Shoshone-Hidatsa woman in order to complete their mission. Sacagawea's husband Toussaint Charbonneau made contact with the expedition's leaders on November 4, 1804, and he appears to have pitched the idea of accompanying the Corps of Discovery, together with one or both of his Shoshone wives, when the expedition resumed its journey towards the Rocky Mountains and Pacific Ocean.

Did Lewis and Clark Meet Omaha Indians in Iowa?

No. On August 13, 1804, Lewis and Clark dispatched Sergeant John Ordway, Pierre Cruzatte, and others to make contact with the Omaha Indians and to invite them to a council on the western bank of the Missouri River. Ordway and his colleagues found their way to the Omaha village of Tonwontonga, which was empty. "Those people," Clark concluded, "have not returned from the Buffalow hunt." Clark reasoned that the ravages of smallpox had severed the Omaha people's ties to their principal village, and that they now spent more time in pursuit of buffalo on the Nebraska plains. The Omaha now had only "the graves of their ancestors to attach them to the old Village," Clark wrote. Lewis and Clark were disappointed ("a great missfortune"), in part because they had hoped to broker a peace agreement between the Omaha and their enemies the Oto and Missouri Indians. Tonwontonga was an earthlodge village in today's Dakota County, Nebraska, just north of the town of Homer, Nebraska.

Were Lewis and Clark Aware of the Impact of Smallpox on the Tribes?

Yes and no. They mention the fact that smallpox had killed the controversial Omaha chief Blackbird in 1800. They report the fact as many as 400 Omaha individuals died in the epidemic, and that some Omaha men put their wives and children to death at the height of the crisis, to help them escape the miasma and insure that they would join their husbands in the next world. They also knew that the Missouri Indians, a once proud and independent tribe, had been so reduced by the disease that they had merged their survivors with the larger remnant population of the Otos.

Living as they did at a time when the white population was periodically decimated by smallpox, and when vaccination was still a rare and controversial procedure, Lewis and Clark fully understood the gravity of the disease. But they knew almost nothing about the human immune system, and the reason for the special susceptibility of Indians to such old world diseases as smallpox.

At the suggestion of President Jefferson's Attorney General Levi Lincoln, the expedition carried smallpox vaccine in its medical kit, with the idea of vaccinating willing Indians along the Missouri River. Unfortunately, the vaccine had become inert long before the expedition got underway, and no serious effort was made to replenish the original supply. The vaccination plan was not a priority.

It is certain that Lewis and Clark felt no cultural responsibility for the impact of smallpox on Indian populations, if the journals are a fair measure of their attitude. They looked upon the devastations of smallpox in the Missouri basin in a matter-of-fact fashion, and they never expressed even a minimal sense of responsibility for the (admittedly unintended) negative impacts of the Euro-American civilization that they so proudly represented. There is no evidence that any participant in the Lewis and Clark expedition carried the disease into the wilderness, though it is certain that some members were responsible for carrying venereal diseases from one individual or tribe to another.

Experiencing Iowa

Why was the Expedition So Eager to Determine Latitude and Longitude?

The Lewis and Clark Expedition was an Enlightenment project. President Jefferson envisioned not a great American adventure into the wilderness, but rather a scientific reconnaissance of the interior of the continent. He saw Lewis and Clark as data-collection agents, and his primary goal was to learn as much as possible about the geography of the American West.

In his instructions of June 20, 1803, Jefferson gave special emphasis to latitude and longitude. "Beginning at the mouth of the Missouri, you will take observations of latitude & longitude, at all remarkable points on the river, & especially at the mouths of rivers, at rapids, at islands & other places & objects distinguished by such natural marks & characters of a durable kind, as that they may with certainty be recognized hereafter." In other words, Jefferson wanted Lewis and Clark to locate key places on the grid of the earth. Determining latitude and longitude would provide a mathematical precision that no descriptive language could equal.

Determining latitude was quite simple in 1804. Longitude involved repeated and painstaking observations, and considerable mathematical cogitation. Although Lewis (and sometimes Clark) dutifully conducted celestial observation throughout the expedition's journey, his data were declared unintelligible by the West Point mathematician who analyzed the data after the expedition's return. As late as 1816, Jefferson was still trying to find ways to get the data into

the hands of a War Department mathematician
so that at least Clark's master map could
be corrected by reference to the celestial
observations of the expedition.

Both Captains had Birthdays During the Iowa Interlude. How Did they Celebrate?

William Clark was born on August 1, 1770
in Caroline County, Virginia. Clark celebrated
his thirty-fourth birthday at the Council Bluff
campsite, on the Nebraska side of the Missouri
River, near today's town of Fort Calhoun,
approximately fifteen miles north of Omaha.
On that day, the expedition made no forward
progress. It was, comparatively, a day of rest,
though the delay was motivated by Indian
diplomacy rather than by Clark's birthday. Clark
requested a special meal in honor of the occasion.
Even so, he made reference to his birthday only in
his field notes, and he chose not to make mention
of the occasion in the finished journal for the day.
"This being my birth day I order'd a Saddle of fat
Vennison, an Elk fleece & a Bevertail to be cooked
and a Desert of Cheries, Plumbs, Raspberries
Currents and grapes of a Supr.quallity," he wrote.

Clark spent part of the day preparing what
he called a "flashey" peace pipe for use in the
upcoming Indian council. He also spent part of
the day observing the rich abundance of flora on
the plains near the mouth of the Platte River. "the
Praries Contain Cheres, Apple, Grapes, Currents,
Rasp burry, Gooseberris Hastlenuts and a great
Variety of Plants & flours not Common too the
U.S," he wrote. "What a field for a Botents and
a natirless." Clark, a notoriously weak speller,
meant that the Council Bluff region would be a
goldmine for a competent botanist or naturalist.

Meriwether Lewis was born in Albemarle County, Virginia, on August 18, 1774. Lewis's thirtieth birthday occurred at what the expedition called Fish Camp, not far from today's Dakota City, Nebraska. It was an extremely busy day on the Lewis and Clark trail. In the fifth of seven courts martial of the expedition, Moses Reed was tried and sentenced for desertion.

Lewis's birthday "was Closed," Clark wrote, "with an extra Gill of Whiskey & a Dance until 11 oClock." Probably the conviviality had more to do with the expedition's desire to entertain the visiting Oto delegation, and the need to reassure the men after what can only have been a day of extraordinary tension, than with Lewis's birthday.

Did Lewis and Clark See Evidence of a Tornado During their Time in Iowa?

Yes. Near the place the expedition designated as the Council Bluff, near today's Fort Calhoun, Nebraska, on July 29, 1804, Clark wrote, "above this high land & on the S.S. passed much falling timber apparently the ravages of a Dreddfull harican which had passed oblequely across the river from N.W. to S.E. about twelve months Since, many trees were broken off near the ground the trunks of which were sound and four feet in Diameter." What Clark called a "harican" (hurricane) was undoubtedly a prairie tornado. Clark believed that the storm had occurred a year prior to the arrival of the expedition.

What Did the Dog Seaman Do in Iowa?

Meriwether Lewis's Newfoundland dog Seaman is never mentioned during the Iowa interlude, not in 1804, not in 1806.

Seaman did play a significant role in the success of the expedition, but the dog is mentioned most frequently in the 1805 season of travel, and principally in Montana.

Lewis had purchased the full-grown Newfoundland dog for $20 in Pittsburgh while he awaited the completion of the expedition's keelboat. The dog's name is now thought to have been Seaman, though for most of the last two hundred years its name was transcribed by Lewis and Clark editors as Scannon.

Did Clark Really Write that the Mosquitos Were as Large as Houseflies?

Yes! Mosquitos were a huge factor in the Lewis and Clark Expedition. At a time when chemical insect repellants did not exist, and no pesticides had yet been concocted, mosquitos were a source of great annoyance and—unbeknownst to Lewis and Clark or even the best medical practitioners in the world—the means by which such diseases as malaria and yellow fever were transmitted. The expedition carried a considerable quantity of mosquito netting, some of which survived almost to the end of the journey, but the journals record an almost continuous lament about the ability of mosquitos to make even intrepid explorers miserable.

In the second year of the expedition, in Montana, Meriwether Lewis wrote of "our trio of pests": prickly pear cactus, gnats, and mosquitos. Lewis considered these pests "equal to any three

curses that ever poor Egypt laiboured under, except the Mohometant yoke."

On Friday, July 27, 1804, at Camp White Catfish in Iowa, William Clark wrote, "a butifull Breeze from the N W. this evening which would have been verry agreeable, had the Misquiters been tolerably Pacifick, but they were rageing all night, Some about the Sise of house flais."

On the return journey, on September 5, 1806, the mosquitos were so oppressive that every member of the expedition was up at the crack of dawn, ready to get underway in the hope that the open river would provide enough breeze to reduce the terrible suffering.

What Were the Moments of Tension in Iowa?

Probably the moment of greatest tension was the sudden death of Sergeant Charles Floyd on August 20, 1804. Such an occurrence, even if statistically predictable, must have sent waves of sorrow, fear, and uncertainty through the ranks of the expedition.

Perhaps equally tense was the court martial of Moses Reed on August 18, 1804. Reed's infraction was serious and his punishment horrific. The captains must have wondered whether Reed's disenchantment was shared by other members of the expedition. They must at least have asked themselves how deep and widespread was discontentment with their leadership. If Reed deserted just four months into the expedition, how many more men would seek to quit before the Corps of Discovery reached the Pacific Ocean? As the men formed a gauntlet through which poor Reed was forced to run four times, each man clubbing Reed with as much force as he wished, they must have experienced a complex of emotions. This situation was further intensified because the Oto and Missouri Indian leaders who witnessed the punishment protested that it was too severe, and petitioned the captains for leniency. Now all the pressures of an internal discipline crisis were exacerbated by a cross-cultural misunderstanding. The "savages" were calling the "civilized" men barbaric!

Another source of tension was the disaffection of an Indian man named Big Blue Eyes at the second Indian council on August 18, 1804. The captains were outraged by Big Blue Eyes's rejection of the paper certificate of good behavior that the expedition presented to him. Clark's language was unusually severe: we "rebuked them verry roughly for having in object goods and not peace with their neighbours. this language they did not like at first, but at length all petitioned for us to give back the Certificate to the Big blue eyes he came forward and made a plausible excuse." As Clark's journal makes clear, the expedition was eventually able to bully Big Blue Eyes into pretending to be satisfied with a printed sheet of paper as a gift of international respect, but even so, the captains must have felt some concern that their diplomatic initiatives might face obstacles that they had not fully anticipated at St. Louis.

In addition to all of this, in Iowa the expedition experienced the anxiety of wanting (and needing) to make contact with Indian tribes, but discovering that their Missouri River villages were deserted while their inhabitants were apparently off to the west on the Nebraska plains on their summer buffalo hunts. Even if the captains

THOMAS JEFFERSON,
PRESIDENT

OF THE UNITED STATES OF AMERICA.

From the powers vested in us and   *by the above authority : To all who shall see these presents, Greeting:*

OW YE, that from the special confidence reposed by us in the sincere and unalterable attachment of

f the   NATION to the UNITED STATES ; as also from the abundant proofs given by him of his ami-

isposition to cultivate peace, harmony, and good neighbourhood with the said States, and the citizens of the same ; we

he authority vested in us, require and charge, all citizens of the United States, all Indian Nations, in treaty with the

and all other persons whomsoever, to   acknowledge, and treat the said   and his

in the most friendly manner, declaring him to be the friend and ally of the said States : the government of which

all times be extended to their protection, so long as they do acknowledge the authority of the same.

Having signed with our hands and affixed our seals

this   day of   180

Printed form used by the Captains during the
Expedition, Clark, William, 1770-1838, Yale Collection
of Western Americana, Beinecke Rare Book and
Manuscript Library

understood that the absence of the Indians
had a rational explanation, they must have felt
concern that President Jefferson's diplomatic
agenda could not be advanced. Attempts to
make contact with the tribes had so far failed. Of
course, the expedition did make contact with the
Oto and the Missouri Indians in what is now Iowa
and Nebraska, first on August 2-3, 1804, and
again on August 18-19.

What Did Clark's Slave York Do in Iowa and Nebraska?

York is mentioned only once. When Sergeant
Charles Floyd became suddenly and gravely ill
on August 18, 1804, Clark noted that all the men
of the expedition were attentive to Floyd, "york
prylly." Lewis and Clark editor Gary Moulton took
this to mean "York principally."

This account of the extraordinary care that
York provided for the stricken Floyd squares with
what we know from other episodes recorded in
the journals. When Sacagawea was indisposed
during the last weeks of her (first) pregnancy
in late January, 1805, at Fort Mandan in what
is now North Dakota, Clark records that he
"ordered my Servent to, give her Some froot
Stewed and tee at dift Tims." When Clark and
the Charbonneau family were caught in a flash
flood at the Great Falls of the Missouri River in
Montana, on June 29, 1805, York was frantic
with worry. When Clark and the Charbonneaus
climbed out of the flooded ravine, Clark wrote, "I
found my servant in serch of us greatly agitated,
for our wellfar."

Although York is sometimes portrayed, without
evidence, as a kind of comic (almost a minstrel)
figure, the textual evidence suggests that he

actually distinguished himself as a kind of nurse of the expedition.

How Much Has the Missouri River Changed Since the Time of Lewis and Clark?

Dramatically. In Thomas Jefferson's time the Missouri River was a raw force of nature. Today it is a creature of the U.S. Army Corps of Engineers.

This transformation is made possible by a series of gigantic mainstem dams between Fort Peck, Montana, and the bottom of South Dakota, and by extensive dredging and channel stabilization between Sioux City, Iowa, and the mouth of the Missouri River near St. Charles, Missouri.

The effect of this change is that the waters that flow along the western edge of Iowa are no longer a natural river. They are deeper, colder, clearer, and more rigidly channelized than the Missouri River waters of 1804.

Undoubtedly Lewis and Clark would recognize today's Missouri River in Iowa, and they would probably approve of the industrialization of the river. Their attitude towards the Missouri River was pragmatic, not romantic. The Missouri was their road to the Pacific Ocean. They regarded it as a difficult and frustrating road, and they would surely have welcomed any industrial activity that made their progress easier and more rapid.

What would surprise Lewis and Clark most is that the Missouri River is no longer the nation's freeway into the American northwest. That role is shared by railroads, the interstate highway system, and air traffic. Today the "mighty and heretofore deemed endless Missouri River" has a dramatically diminished role in the nation's infrastructure.

What Are the Mysteries of the Lewis and Clark Expedition in Iowa?

There are several.

Why did the captains decide not to send a map and dispatches back to President Jefferson from the mouth of the Platte River? That they intended to dispatch Corporal Warfington and his crew from the mouth of the Platte with such documents is certain. On July 23, 1804, at Camp White Catfish, Clark wrote, "I commenced Coppying my map of the river to Send to the Presdt. of U S. by the Return of a pty of Soldiers, from Illinois." A day later he wrote, "Capt. Lewis also much engaged in prepareing Papers to Send back by a Pirogue." The busy captains would not have taken the time to prepare these materials just north of the mouth of the Platte unless they believed, right up till the last moment, that a boat would be sent downriver from the confluence. For some reason, the dispatch mission was canceled at the last minute, and neither captain explained their reasons for the decision. It may be that finishing the intended reports proved to be too time consuming during prime traveling season. Also on a number of other occasions during the expedition, Meriwether Lewis expressed concern that sending any fraction of his men back to civilization before the expedition completed its mission might "defeat the expedition altogether."

Meriwether Lewis's silence has perplexed all students of the expedition. Although President Jefferson clearly instructed his protégé to keep a daily record of his travels, Lewis appears to have failed to keep a journal for well over half of his transcontinental journey. Lewis was mostly silent during the Iowa interlude both in 1804 and 1806. He was a very busy man throughout the voyage— collecting and pressing plants, attempting to determine latitude and longitude, describing new or unusual animals, reflecting on the geopolitical implications of his mission—but Clark was equally busy and he almost never failed to write a journal entry. Some historians have speculated that Lewis was keeping a journal during the first year of travel and that it was either lost in a boat accident or misplaced at the time of his sudden death in 1809. The evidence from the journals, however, suggests that Lewis was indeed silent for extended periods of time, and that at some early point he and Clark determined that if one of them was keeping a daily narrative of the expedition's activities, that would serve as a kind of "captains' log," in compliance with President Jefferson's instructions.

Who was Mr. Fairfong? On August 2, 1804, a small delegation of Oto and Missouri Indians approached the expedition's camp at Council Bluff with a French trader whom Clark called "Mr. Fairfong." Attempts to identify this individual have ended in frustration. All we know is that Fairfong was a resident trader among the Oto and Missouri Indians, that he provided the expedition with considerable information about Indian language groups and Platte River geography, and that he knew something about the trade route between the Platte River and Santa Fe. The captains appreciated Fairfong's efforts enough to give him a parcel of goods before they resumed their journey.

What do we know about the desertion of Moses Reed?

Almost nothing is known about the biography of Moses Reed. He was a permanent member of the expedition until his court martial on August 18, 1804. Where he was born, how old he was, what his previous occupations had been, and just when he joined the expedition, are all unknown. Nor is much known about Reed after his return to St. Louis in the keelboat in the spring of 1805. Clark did not mention Reed at all in his (1825-1828) tallying of the post-expeditionary fate of individual members.

The French *engagé* La Liberté deserted the expedition while on an official diplomatic mission to the Missouri and Oto villages. The army private Moses Reed initiated his desertion by claiming that he had left his knife in the previous camp, and getting permission to go back for it.

Reed's desertion was not taken lightly. His protracted absence was first noticed by William Clark on August 4, 1804. "Reed a man who went back to Camp for his knife has not joined us." One day later Clark wrote, "The man who went back after his Knife has not yet come up, we have Some reasons to believe he has Deserted." Sergeant Charles Floyd indicated the reasons in his journal: "pon examining his nap-Sack we found that he had taken his Cloas and all His powder and Balles, and had hid them out that night and had made that an excuse to Desarte from us with out aney Jest Case."

On August 6, the captains took action. "We have every reason to belive that one man has Deserted Moses B: Reed he has been absent three Days and one french man we Sent to the

Indian Camps has not joined us, we have reasons to beleve he lost himself in attempting to join us at the Council Bluff-- we are deturmind to Send back 4 men to take reede Dead or alive."

The search party, led by the expedition's indispensable man George Drouillard, was gone ten days on its search for Moses Reed. He represents one of the principal diversions of energy of the entire Lewis and Clark Expedition.

On August 16, one member of the "posse," Labiche, returned to report that the others were on their way to camp with Reed, who had been successfully apprehended, but not with La Liberté, who had somehow managed to slip away. Labiche also reported that a delegation of Oto leaders was accompanying the "posse." Once everyone was safely in camp, the captains postponed the council with the Oto leaders until Reed had been officially dealt with. In this instance, military discipline and the *esprit de corps* of the expedition were seen as more important (or at least more immediately important) than the Indian peace and trade agenda of the Corps of Discovery.

Reed was tried by court martial on August 18, 1804, Meriwether Lewis's 30th birthday. He was sentenced to run the gauntlet four times and punished the same day. According to Robert Moore, an expert on military aspects of the expedition, the gauntlet was an exceedingly brutal form of punishment which could inflict serious and possibly permanent damage on the victim. The men of the gauntlet were permitted, indeed encouraged, to beat the victim as hard as they wished with the implements at hand – in this case "each man with 9 Swichies," as Clark described it.

This judicial beating took place a few miles south of today's Dakota City, Nebraska.

Although he was discharged, Reed accompanied the expedition to its winter quarters in today's North Dakota, assigned to the most onerous and undignified labors of the expedition, until he was permitted to return to civilization on the keelboat beginning April 7, 1805. Thus Moses Reed's immortality is that he was the Lewis and Clark Expedition's only official deserter. (The French *engagé* La Liberté abandoned the expedition sometime after July 29, 1804, but since he was not enlisted in the U.S. Army, his disappearance is not usually regarded as an official desertion. Certainly the captains considered La Liberté's offense as distinct and inferior to Reed's action).

The Death of Charles Floyd

What do we know about Charles Floyd?

Floyd was one of the so-called Nine Young Men from Kentucky. Born in Kentucky in 1782, Floyd was just twenty-two years old at the time of the expedition's departure. Some historians believe that he was a distant cousin of William Clark.

Floyd was one of the three sergeants designated by the captains. His sudden death produced a vacuum in the leadership of the expedition, filled by the democratic election of Patrick Gass as sergeant on August 22, 1804. The election, sometimes called the first

Opposite page: Clark-Maximilian pictographic drawing, sheet 5: Route about August 13-21, 1804, Joslyn Art Museum, Omaha, Nebraska

Cobalt, Pyrites, Copperas, & Alum Bluff

Ancient Village of the
Mahars

So
a

Bam
Floyd's River

Sergent C. Floyd was
20th of August 1803

Camped 13th, 14th, 15th, 16th
and 17th of August 1804
Latitude 42° 13' 41" N.

ling House

democratic election in the Louisiana Territory, took place just inside today's South Dakota.

Floyd's first and only mention of his deteriorating health came on July 31, 1804, at the Council Bluff. "I am verry Sick and Has ben for Somtime but have Recoverd my helth again." After that, Floyd resumes his daily notes on the events of the expedition. Floyd's journal, from May 14 until August 18, 1804, two days before his death, is the crudest and least literate of all surviving original journals.

Both captains wrote favorably of Charles Floyd. In 1807 Lewis described him as "a young man of much merit," and urged the U.S. War Department to provide compensation to Floyd's father: "As the son has lost his life while on this service, I consider his father entitled to some gratuity, in consideration of his loss." On the day of Floyd's death, Clark wrote movingly that "This Man at all times gave us proofs of his firmness and Deturmined resolution to doe Service to his Countrey and honor to himself."

How did Floyd Die?

Learned opinions vary. The consensus has been that Floyd died of a ruptured appendix. Recent scholarship has cast doubt on this diagnosis, however. We know for sure only that Floyd's malady was sudden, devastating, and untreatable by the medical procedures of the age. Every commentator agrees that Floyd would almost certainly have perished in Louisville, Philadelphia (the center of American medicine), or Edinburgh (the center of medicine in the English-speaking world). Clark called his malady "Beliose Chorlick," but no autopsy was conducted and no serious examination was made of Floyd's body before he was buried. He died around noon on August 20, 1804, and by sundown he had been buried on a bluff a few miles upriver.

In a brilliant analysis of the sketchy evidence from the journals, Dr. Bruce C. Paton casts serious doubt on the notion that Floyd died of a ruptured appendix. Although Paton believes that the evidence does not permit a conclusive identification of the malady that killed Floyd, he inclines to a massive intestinal infection.

Dr. David Peck devotes much of his analysis to a discussion of the early nineteenth-century medical care that Lewis and Clark administered to poor Floyd, which almost certainly made matters worse rather than better. In the end, Peck calls appendicitis the "leading candidate."

It is important to note that Floyd was ill twice in the last month of his life. Floyd wrote in his journal on July 31, 1804, that he was recovering from a serious illness that he had experienced for some period, in other words, for days if not weeks. This was, in fact, Floyd's only mention of illness in his journal. The second bout of illness, possibly related, possibly distinct, was so potent and it came on so fast that Floyd did not have time to make mention of it in his journal. Every other journal-keeper, however, described what happened. John Ordway reported that "Sgt. Floyd taken verry Sudenly Ill this morning with a collick." Clark wrote that Floyd was "taken verry bad all at once."

It is not clear whether these were two flare-ups of the same illness, the second of which killed Floyd, or rather two distinct illnesses, the first of which weakened Floyd's immune system, and the second of which killed him.

How Did the Last Hours of Charles Floyd's Life Unfold?

Floyd's second, and final, illness first attracted notice on Sunday, August 19, 1804. It was an exceedingly busy day. Moses Reed was just beginning to recover from the severe beating he had received on August 18. The expedition held the second of the two councils it conducted with representatives of the Oto and Missouri Indians. At the end of his field note journal entry for the day, Clark turned his attention to the stricken Floyd: "Sergt. Floyd was taken violently bad with the Beliose Cholick and is dangerously ill we attempt in Vain to releive him, I am much concerned for his Situation-- we could get nothing to Stay on his Stomach a moment nature appear exosting fast in him every man is attentive to him <york prily>" In his formal journal entry for the day, Clark wrote, "we are muc allarmed at his Situation."

Floyd's own last journal entry had occurred on August 18, though it had mentioned nothing about his illness. On August 19, John Ordway wrote, "Sgt. Floyd taken verry Sudenly Ill this morning with a collick." Gass and Whitehouse made virtually identical comments.

On Sunday, August 20, the expedition started out as usual, but Floyd was now a stricken passenger rather than a waterman. Clark wrote, "I am Dull & heavy been up the greater Part of last night with Serjt. Floyd, who is a bad as he can be to live the of his bowels having changed &c. is the Cause of his violent attack &c. &c." At noon on that day, "we Came to make a warm bath for Sergt. Floyd hopeing it would brace him a little, before we could get him in to his bath he expired, with a great deel of composure." Joseph Whitehouse wrote, "The disease which occasion'd his death . . . baffled all medical aid, that Captain Lewis could administer."

Just before he died, Floyd told captain Clark "that he was going away and wished me to write a letter--" Nobody knows whether he lived long enough to dictate the letter to Clark.

After Floyd died, the expedition continued up river a couple of miles in search of a proper place to inter his body. "we Buried him to the top of a high round hill over looking the river & Countrey for a great distance," Clark wrote. "Situated just below a Small river without a name to which we name & call Floyds river, the Bluffs Sergts. Floyds Bluff."

After the funeral, the expedition proceeded on a short distance to the mouth of Floyd's River, and formed a camp.

What Was Floyd's Funeral Like?

The details are maddeningly sparse.

Although Charles Floyd died on the Missouri River at about noon on August 20, 1804, he was buried several hours later on a bluff overlooking the river from the east, at today's Sioux City, Iowa.

"[H]e was laid out in the Best Manner possible," John Ordway wrote. Presumably this means that Floyd was groomed as much as possible under the circumstances and that his body was positioned (perhaps on a board?) in a dignified manner. Then Floyd's body was carried by his peers up what Clark called "Sergts. Floyds Bluff," where "we dug the Grave on a handsome Sightly Round knob close to the Bank." Historians have disagreed about whether the expedition, perhaps led by carpenter Patrick Gass, fashioned a makeshift casket for Floyd. The expedition's journals are entirely silent on this question. Was Floyd's body draped in one of the expedition's fifteen-star American flags? Nobody knows.

Ordway reported that "we buried him with the honours of war. the usal Serrymony performed (by Capt. Lewis as customommary in a Settlement." By Settlement Ordway means a frontier community.

A red cedar post was fixed at the head of Floyd's grave. It was branded with the words, "Sergt. C. Floyd died here 20th of august 1804."

Is Sergeant Floyd Buried Where Lewis and Clark Left Him?

No. The current monument, erected in 1901, was built over the fourth grave of Charles Floyd.

Floyd was originally buried on the day he died, August 20, 1804, on a bluff a few miles upriver from where he drew his final breath, near the mouth of Floyd's River, which was named that day in his honor. A cedar post was erected atop the grave. By the time the expedition returned to Iowa in 1806, Indians had tampered with the grave. Lewis and Clark restored the integrity of the burial site before resuming their downriver journey.

By 1857, erosion had exposed Floyd's grave and scattered some of his remains. His skull was found at the base of the bluff by the Missouri's shore. At that time, Floyd's remains were collected and reburied about six hundred feet away from the original gravesite.

Floyd was reburied at the same site again on August 20, 1895, on the ninety-first anniversary of his death. A marble slab was placed on the site.

Floyd's final burial occurred on August 20, 1900, when the cornerstone was laid for what became the 100-foot sandstone obelisk that now overlooks the Missouri River at Sioux, City, Iowa. At that time, Floyd's bones were placed in the core of the monument. Since then, Floyd has rested in peace.

How Was Floyd Replaced as One of the Expedition's Sergeants?

The Corps of Discovery held an election on August 22, 1804, in what is now South Dakota to replace Floyd. Private Patrick Gass won the election with nineteen votes. William Bratton and George Gibson and unnamed others split the rest of the votes, though the exact figures are not recorded in Clark's journal. The vote took place in today's Union County, South Dakota, near the town of Elk Point.

Going Home

What Was the Mood of the Expedition During the Return Journey in 1806?

If on the upriver journey of 1804, the expedition was characterized by optimism, testosterone, high spirits, eagerness to make contact with Indian nations, scientific zeal, and a sense of the transcontinental mission that President Jefferson had ordered, by the time the Corps of Discovery returned to Iowa in 1806 the energies that had launched the expedition were exhausted. The men of the expedition, particularly Meriwether Lewis, were impatient with Indians and they wanted to have as little contact with Missouri River tribes as possible.

Lewis and Clark rushed through Iowa in 1806 and they saw the gorgeous prairie landscape not

20th August Monday 180[ ]

Sergeant Floyd much weake[r]
and no better. Made Mr. Fa[ ]
the interpeter a few presents, [ ]
the Indians a Canister of W[ ]
we Set out under a gentle b[reeze]
from the S.E. and proceeded [ ]
very well – Sergeant Floyd
bad as he can be no pul[se]
nothing) will Stay amon[g]
[i]n his Stomach or bowels –
Passed two Islands on the s[ ]
[a]nd at the first Bluff on [ ]
[S.]S. Serg[t.] Floyd Died with a
[g]reat deal of Composure, b[efore]
[h]is death he Said to me "I[am]
[g]oing away" I want you to wri[te]
[m]e a letter" – We buried hi[m]
[o]n the top of the bluff ½ Mile
[b]elow a Smale river to which
[g]ave his name, he was bur[ied]
[w]ith the Honors of war muc[h]

Lewis and Clark Codex B: 13–14 (death of Floyd)
American Philosophical Society

58

emented, a Ceeder post with h[is]
[n]ame Serg.t C. Floyd deed here 20 A[u]
[u]gust 1804 was fixed at the [h]
[ea]d of his grave — this Man
[at] all times gave us proofs of
[hi]s firmness and Determined
[re]solution to doe Service to his
[Cou]ntrey and honor to himself
[Af]ter paying all the honor [to]
[ou]r Deceised brother we Camp[ed at]
the Mouth of floyds river [a]
[b]out 30 yards wide, a beut[iful]
[ev]ening). —

[C]ourse Dist.s & reffr 20.th Aug.t

56.° W.	3 M.s to pt. of a willow Is.d S.S.
[N] orth.	3/4 M.s on the left of the Isla[nd]
72. E.	2 1/4 M.s to the upr. pt. of the [I.]
18. E	2 1/2 M.s to the lower pt. of an[d]
	Is.o on the S.S. passed Sand [I.]
th 3 1/2 M.r	[op]ste Sgt. Floyds Bluff on S[S.]
	the 1.st above arraways Villag[e]
	a few Miles above Platt[e]
1 1/2	To the Mo: of Floyds River
13 3/4	on S.S. & camped

as an American Garden of Eden or a platform for future Jeffersonian farms, or an arena in which to pursue President Jefferson's geopolitical objectives, but merely as the measure of the space and time that separated them, in Lewis's words, from all that they held estimable in life.

It was time to go home.

What Did Lewis and Clark Know of the World to Which They Were Returning?

Just as they were about to enter Iowa, on September 3, 1806, below the mouth of the Vermillion River, Lewis and Clark met the first of the half dozen or so traders they would encounter between the bottom of South Dakota and St. Louis. In command of the small cluster of commercial boats was James Aird, a Scottish national who had an American license to trade with the Sioux. Lewis and Clark met his boats at 4:30 p.m. They quickly agreed to share a campsite for the night.

Desperate for news, the captains pumped Aird with questions: "our first enquirey was after the President of our country and then our friends and the State of the politicks of our country &c. and the State of Indian affairs."

It was a violently stormy night, and Clark found shelter in Aird's tent in part to get out of the rain, and in part to pry more information out of the trader. Aird informed Clark that the house of the expedition's friend Jean Pierre Chouteau had burned down in St. Louis; that there were international difficulties with the Spanish both in lower Louisiana and on the high seas, in addition to tensions between the United States and Great Britain; that James Wilkinson was the Governor of Louisiana; that two Kickapoo individuals had been hanged in St. Louis for the murder of an unidentified white man on a prairie near the Osage River; and that Thomas Jefferson's political adversary Alexander Hamilton was dead, cut down in a duel by Vice President Aaron Burr. In short, the world had carried on in the absence of Lewis and Clark and the Scottish trader had compelling news to report.

The Last Five Days in Today's Iowa

On Thursday, **September 4**, after saying farewell to James Aird and accepting his gift of a barrel of flour and enough tobacco to get the men home to St. Louis, the expedition proceeded on to Floyd's Bluff. Although Meriwether Lewis was still recovering from his gunshot wounds, he was fit enough to climb the hill to Charles Floyd's grave as a gesture of respect to the only white casualty of the Lewis and Clark Expedition. Floyd's grave had been tampered with. Clark believed that "the grave had been opened by the nativs and left half Covered." The captains and their small party restored the integrity of the grave and returned to the river. The expedition made camp at Fish Camp, on the Nebraska shore, which had been the campsite of the expedition between August 13 and 20, 1804. The captains issued each man a "cup of flour," by way of a treat. The expedition had traveled just thirty-six miles that day.

On Friday, **September 5**, fierce attacks by mosquitos inspired everyone to man the boats earlier than usual! Nothing of particular importance happened that day. The comparative leisure allowed William Clark to comment on the geomorphology of the Missouri River.

The expedition concluded that gunshots it had heard the previous night had been fired by the Omaha Indians with whom the expedition had failed to make contact in 1804, but nobody seemed interested in pausing to make contact with a tribe that had been a key part of the expedition's diplomatic agenda just two years previously.

On Saturday, **September 6**, the Lewis and Clark expedition tasted whiskey for the first time in 429 days. Near the mouth of the Little Sioux River the expedition encountered a trading party led by a man named Henry Delorn, an employee of Rene Auguste Chouteau. The captains purchased a gallon of whiskey for the men. Several expedition individuals engaged in some private trade: their buckskins for linen shirts, their beaver hats for coarse cloth hats.

On Sunday, **September 7**, after several days of poor hunting the expedition managed to kill three elk, which provided what Clark called "a Sumptious Dinner." The mosquitos were "excessively tormenting not withstanding a Stiff breeze from the S.E." The expedition traveled forty-four miles and camped a little below its campsite of August 4, 1804—near today's Blair, Nebraska.

On Monday, **September 8**, the expedition's penultimate day in Iowa, hard rowing carried the flotilla seventy-eight miles, almost to the mouth of the Platte River. The expedition spent the night at Camp White Catfish (the home of the expedition from July 22-26, 1804). For the second day in a row, Clark mused about the remarkable evaporation rate of the Missouri River: "The Missouri at this place does not appear to

Contain more water than it did 1000 Miles above this, the evaperation must be emence; in the last 1000 miles this river receives the water 20 rivers and maney Creeks Several of the Rivers large and the Size of this river or the quantity of water does not appear to increas any—[.]"

Finally, on Tuesday, **September 9**, 1806, the Lewis and Clark Expedition passed the "great river Platt" without fanfare, and camped outside the boundaries of today's Iowa, at the "Bald pated prairie" on the Missouri side of the border. The expedition had covered a distance of seventy-three miles between 8 a.m. and "late in the evening." "our party," Clark wrote, "appears extreamly anxious to get on, and every day appears produce new anxieties in them to get to their Country and friends." The best news of the day is that Meriwether Lewis had entirely recovered from the shooting that occurred twenty-nine days previously, on August 11, 1806. "My worthy friend Cap Lewis has entirely recovered his wounds are heeled up and he Can walk and even run nearly as well as ever he Could. the parts are yet tender &c. &."

What Was the Aftermath of the Lewis and Clark Expedition?

The Corps of Discovery returned to St. Louis on September 23, 1806. The men were paid off and the surplus equipment was unceremoniously sold off. The captains made their way back to Virginia and Washington, D.C.—national heroes at a time when the American media was largely incapable of trumpeting their achievement. The Enlightenment president Thomas Jefferson was mighty glad to see his protégé Lewis, and he arranged for generous compensation packages for the captains and their men. Lewis was appointed Governor of Upper Louisiana. Clark was made a Brigadier General in the militia and the superintendent of Indian affairs at St. Louis. Jefferson encouraged Lewis to publish his three-volume account of the expedition as soon as possible.

Clark thrived. Lewis fell into steep decline. Clark married Julia Hancock and began to produce offspring. Lewis described himself as a fusty, musty, rusty old bachelor. Clark was able to get along with practically everyone. Lewis made enemies just about as fast as he had collected plant specimens in the wilderness. His subordinate in St. Louis said Lewis should never have resigned from the army. He was, said Frederick Bates, fitted for military command, but he had insufficient flexibility of character to tolerate the yeasty stuff of frontier democracy.

Above all, Lewis could not finish his book. He lied about his progress, and stopped answering President Jefferson's letters. At the time of his death, so far as we know, he had not written a single page of his proposed three-volume narrative.

Lewis died from gunshot wounds, probably self-inflicted, on the Natchez Trace, in the early morning hours of October 11, 1809. He was thirty-five years old. Only three years had passed since his triumphant return from the Pacific Ocean.

Clark lived a full, productive, and by all accounts happy life. He had two wives and seven children, the first of whom he named Meriwether Lewis Clark. Clark played an immensely important role in Indian affairs in the Louisiana Purchase country. Somehow he won the respect and even admiration of the Indians he helped to dispossess of their lands. Clark died of natural causes on September 1, 1838 at the age of sixty-eight. Clark's funeral was the largest ever held up til that time in St. Louis.

Sacagawea almost certainly died young, approximately twenty-five years old, of "putrid fever," near what became the North Dakota-South Dakota border. She could not know that she would eventually rival the captains themselves for centrality in the Lewis and Clark mythology. Her colorful and rascally husband Charbonneau lived into doddering old age, collecting young Indian wives along the way. York was finally freed by a reluctant William Clark a few years after the expedition. He went into the freight business. He appears to have died of cholera in Tennessee sometime around 1832, a free man before the coming of Abraham Lincoln.

The last surviving member of the Lewis and Clark Expedition was Sergeant Patrick Gass, who died on April 2, 1870 in West Virginia. He was 99 years old. Gass, who had published the first booklength account of the expedition in 1807, lived long enough to be photographed (as did Alexander Hamilton Willard, another member of the expedition).

Most important of all, the journals of the expedition were finally published in 1814, eight years after the expedition's return, in a somewhat disappointing paraphrase form, denuded of all the serious science. The original journals were not published until the twentieth century. By then, Meriwether Lewis's massive scientific achievement was old news.

What Should I Read about Lewis and Clark in Iowa?

Volumes two and eight of Gary Moulton's *The Journals of the Lewis and Clark Expedition* are indispensable. Professor Moulton has established the standard national text of the journals and his annotations are the starting point for any further study of Lewis and Clark.

James Ronda's, *Lewis and Clark Among the Indians* remains the most important interpretative study ever made of the Lewis and Clark Expedition. Ronda has a long and thoughtful chapter on the first Indian councils of the expedition, which occurred along the Iowa-Nebraska corridor.

Albert Furtwangler's *Acts of Discovery: Visions of America in the Lewis and Clark Journals* provides an insightful account of the ways in which Lewis and Clark came to terms with the landscape of the midwestern prairies and the Great Plains.

The two best general narratives of the expedition are Stephen Ambrose's *Undaunted Courage: Meriwether Lewis, Thomas Jefferson, and the Opening of the American West* and David Lavender's *The Way to the Western Sea: Lewis and Clark across the Continent*.

Useful, too, are Stephenie Ambrose Tubbs's and Clay Jenkinson's *Lewis and Clark Companion* and Elin Woodger and Brandon Toropov's *The Lewis & Clark Encyclopedia*.

Carolyn Gilman's *Lewis and Clark Across the Divide* would rank as the finest coffee table book ever produced about Lewis and Clark were it not for the fact that Ms. Gilman has also written a brilliant and insightful synthesis of the best current understandings of the Lewis and Clark Expedition. In other words, her book is indispensable even without the gorgeous illustrations.

For medical explanation regarding the death of Sergeant Floyd see Bruce Paton's *Lewis & Clark: Doctors in the Wilderness* or David J. Peck's *Or Perish in the Attempt: Wilderness Medicine in the Lewis & Clark Expedition.*

How Can I Experience the Lewis and Clark Expedition in Iowa and Nebraska Today?

Sioux City, Iowa, is one of the handful of Lewis and Clark-related communities across the nation that students of the expedition must not avoid.

The **Sergeant Floyd Monument** in Sioux City is the largest and most prominent monument to any member of the Lewis and Clark Expedition. It overlooks the Missouri River not far from where Charles Floyd died on August 20, 1804.

The new **Sioux City Lewis & Clark Interpretive Center** features animatronic historical characters as Lewis, Clark, Seaman, and a prairie dog, outstanding larger than life sculptures, and historically accurate interpretive panels and exhibits.

At the nearby **Southern Hills Mall**, a series of thirty-eight outstanding murals envelops the central court, depicting scenes from throughout the Corps of Discovery's 7689 mile journey, including the death of Charles Floyd.

Again, the Corps learned how much the Missouri meandered when, after traveling 18 3/4 miles around a loop on August 12, 1804, one man paced off 974 yards to the previous night's

campsite. This loop is now **Badger Lake**, also
known as **Whiting Access**.

Fort Atkinson State Park, in Fort Calhoun,
Nebraska, is located approximately where Lewis
and Clark held their first Indian council on August
3, 1804.

Lewis and Clark State Park at Onawa
contains reconstructions of the expedition's
keelboat and pirogues.

Lewis & Clark camped near the **DeSoto
National Wildlife Refuge** on August 3, the day
of their first council with Indians on the west
side of the river. The refuge is a stopover for the
migration of snow geese and other birds, such
as eagles.

Wilson Island Recreation Area in Missouri
Valley is the site where one of the Corps
members killed a white heron, which was
studied and fully described by Captain Lewis.

Lewis and Clark Monument Overlook
honoring Lewis & Clark sits atop a bluff north of
Council Bluffs and offers vistas of the Council
Bluffs/Omaha metro area and the Missouri River
valley.

Built in 1997 by the National Park Service,
the **Western Historic Trails Center** features
an exhibit hall, a 14 foot Lewis and Clark Icon,
and exhibits along 400 acres of Missouri River
bottom interpreting the voyage, Camp White
Catfish, and Missouri trade history.

After passing the Platte River, the Corps of
Discovery paused on July 22 in a shaded area
in present-day **Lake Manawa State Park** to
dry and repair equipment. Called Camp White
Catfish because Silas Goodrich caught a white

catfish here; this five-day rest was the longest the men had since setting out.

Lewis & Clark Icon Interpretive Sculpture Project near Omaha and Council Bluffs is comprised of two six-piece and six single-piece sculptures interpreting the Voyage of Discovery along the Missouri Riverfront Trails in Iowa and Nebraska.

The confluence of the Platte and Missouri Rivers is best seen just north of the city of Plattsmouth at the **Schilling Wildlife Management Area**.

The **Missouri River Basin Lewis and Clark Interpretive Trail and Visitor Center** in Nebraska City is a 12,000 square foot interpretive center to be completed in July of 2004 with education themes focusing on the 178 plants, animals, and scientific discoveries of the voyage

Located in the Loess Hills, **Waubonsie State Park** features an endless prairie and what Clark described in his journal as "Ball pated" hills.

The **Loess Hills National Scenic Byway**, provides glimpses of what the landscape must have looked like when Lewis and Clark came through in 1804.

For more detailed information, readers should refer to Barbara Fifer and Vicky Soderbert's *Along the Trail with Lewis and Clark* and Julie Faneslow's *Traveling the Lewis and Clark Trail*.

About Clay S. Jenkinson

Clay Jenkinson is a North Dakotan. He is the author of three books on the Lewis and Clark Expedition, most recently *A Vast and Open Plain: The Writings of the Lewis and Clark Expedition in North Dakota*.

Mr. Jenkinson is a humanities scholar in residence at Lewis & Clark College in Portland, Oregon, and a recipient of the National Humanities Medal. He is considered the nation's leading historical interpreter of Thomas Jefferson and Meriwether Lewis, among others.

About Humanities Iowa

Established in 1971, Humanities Iowa is a private, non-profit state affiliate of the National Endowment for the Humanities, whose mission is to enhance the civic life, culture, and identity of Iowans. Drawing on history, literature, philosophy, law, and other humanities fields, it fosters life-long learning, critical thinking, and community connections.

About the Iowa Lewis & Clark Bicentennial Commission

The Iowa Lewis and Clark Commission was established by the Iowa Legislature in the year 2000. The Commission's mission is to create awareness and participation in the bicentennial observance of the Lewis and Clark expedition in 1804-06 and through collaboration, produce programs and materials that reflect the Euro-American and Native American perspectives to create a lasting legacy of Lewis and Clark in Iowa.